THE
MARGINALIA
FAN'S
POCKET JOURNAL

The Marginalia Fan's Pocket Journal
A Fill-In Book for Readers Who Write in the Margins

Part of The Fan's Pocket Journal Series

By Leaves of Gold Press
Edited by C. Egan

ISBN: 978-1-923212-51-0 (paperback)

Series: The fan's pocket journal

Dewey: 808.8

BISAC
LAN009000 LANGUAGE ARTS & DISCIPLINES / Reading Skills

CRA028000 CRAFTS & HOBBIES / Journals

Copyright (C) 2025 Leaves of Gold Press
ABN 67 099 575 078
PO Box 345, Shoreham, 3916, Victoria, Australia

THE MARGINALIA FAN'S POCKET JOURNAL

A Fill-In Book for Readers Who Write in the Margins

Part of The Fan's Pocket Journal Series

The Fan's Pocket Journal Series:

The Marginalia Fan's Pocket Journal

The Magic Academy Fan's Pocket Journal

The #BookTalk & #BookGram Fan's Pocket Journal

The Romantasy Fan's Pocket Journal

. . . and many more!

For readers who know the story isn't finished
until the margins speak.

How to Use This Journal

This is not a review log. It's not homework. It's a place to capture the way you interact with books—the quotes you underline, the doodles you add, the questions you argue with in the margins.

Each page gives you a prompt. Some invite you to write, some to draw, some to swatch your favourite pens or highlighters. There's no wrong way to use them. Skip around, fill them out of order, leave pages half-finished. It's all part of your annotator style.

Think of it as a companion to your books. Where the margins stop, this journal begins.

And if you share your pages online, don't forget: margins are the new "art canvas".

CONTENTS

Chapter One: My Annotator Identity

– Colour codes and annotation styles

Chapter Two: Quote Collecting

– Lines underlined and margin reactions

Chapter Three: Talking Back to Books

– Disagreements and comebacks

Chapter Four: Margin Emotions

– Laughs and tears in the margins

Chapter Five: Symbols and Shortcuts

– Favourite doodles and invented icons

Chapter Six: My Annotator Aesthetic

– Colour palettes and decorated pages

Chapter Seven: Other People's Margins

– Funniest notes and what others would say

Chapter Eight: Books That Became Rainbows

– Most colourful books and favourite spreads

Chapter Nine: Collector's Pages

– Favourite annotated quotes and dream designs

Chapter Ten: Legacy in the Margins

– What future readers will learn and why we annotate

CHAPTER ONE:
MY ANNOTATOR IDENTITY

My Colour-Coding System

Fill in your go-to colours and what they mean. Swatch them here to test your pens and highlighters.

Colour: _____ → Means: _____

Colour: _____ → Means: _____

Colour: _____ → Means: _____

Colour: _____ → Means: _____

Colour: _____ → Means: _____

Colour: _____ → Means: _____

Notes: _____

_____

Share your colour code → #MarginaliaMania

The Kind of Annotator I Am

Some readers highlight everything, some doodle stars, some write essays in the margins. Describe your style here.

_____

_____

_____

_____

_____

Sketch your annotator aesthetic (messy, neat, colourful, chaotic…)

My First Ever Annotation

The very first time I wrote in a book, I noted/doodled…

_____

_____

_____

_____

_____

_____

Recreate it here (quote, doodle, or reaction).

CHAPTER TWO:
QUOTE COLLECTING

❝❝ A Line I Underlined Recently Was...

Copy down a sentence or passage that stopped you in your tracks.

```
_____

_____

_____

_____

_____

_____

_____

_____

_____

_____

_____

_____
```

Don't forget the page number!

My Margin Reaction to It Was...

What did you scribble, sketch, or shout in the margin?

_____

_____

_____

_____

_____

Draw your reaction (exclamation, heart, eye-roll, etc.).

The Quote I Keep Coming Back To

Some lines stay with us, no matter how many books we read. Write down the one you return to most often.

_____

_____

_____

_____

_____

_____

_____

_____

_____

_____

_____

Why it matters to me...

Post this quote + your reaction → #AnnotatorsOfTikTok

CHAPTER THREE:
TALKING BACK TO BOOKS

66 A Passage I Disagreed With

The line that made me argue in the margins was…

_____

_____

_____

_____

_____

_____

_____

What I thought when I read it…

_____

_____

_____

_____

_____

My Sharpest Margin Comeback !

The best one-liner I've ever written in the margin was...

_____

_____

_____

_____

_____

_____

Sketch the mood (angry, sarcastic, playful).

The Margin Note I Wish the Author Could Read

If the writer could see one of my annotations, it would be this one...

_____

_____

_____

_____

_____

_____

Sketch the author's reaction!

Ever fought with a book? Share it → #TalkingBackToBooks

Chapter Four:
Margin Emotions

☺ A Line That Made Me Laugh

Some books sneak in humour where you least expect it. Copy the line here.

_____

_____

_____

_____

_____

_____

Sketch the reaction (smile, doodle, giggle marks).

A Line That Made Me Cry

The passage that broke your heart — write it down before the tears blur it.

The Emotion That Surprised Me Most

Sometimes a book makes us feel something we didn't expect. Write the moment and the feeling it stirred.

_____

_____

_____

_____

_____

_____

Colour it in with the mood (warm, cold, dark, bright).

CHAPTER FIVE:
SYMBOLS AND SHORTCUTS

☆ My Most-Used Doodle or Symbol

Some readers draw stars, hearts, or arrows beside favourite lines. What's your go-to doodle?

I use this doodle when...

_____

_____

_____

_____

_____

_____

_____

My New Annotation Icon

Invent a brand-new symbol. What does it look like, and what does it mean?

Sketch it here: _____

Name of symbol: _____

It means: _____

Where would you use this new symbol?

⟹ The Shortcut I Use Most Often

Some readers use arrows, abbreviations, or quick marks.
Write (or draw) your favourite shortcut.

Description:

_____

_____

_____

_____

_____

Show how it looks in the margin.

Share your doodle language → #PrettyMargins

CHAPTER SIX:
MY ANNOTATOR AESTHETIC

The Highlight Colour Combo I Love Most

Some colours just look perfect together. Swatch your favourite combination here.

Colour: _____ Mood: _____	Colour: _____ Mood: _____
Colour: _____ Mood: _____	Colour: _____ Mood: _____
Colour: _____ Mood: _____	Colour: _____ Mood: _____
Colour: _____ Mood: _____	Colour: _____ Mood: _____

Try layering or pairing them.

A Decorated Margin I'm Proud Of

Sometimes a margin turns into a little artwork of its own. Recreate one you love here.

Book + page number:_____

Margins are the new canvas → #MyMarginNotes

My Ideal Margin Aesthetic

If my margins always looked like this, I'd be happy...

_____

_____

_____

_____

_____

Sketch or pattern it here.

Chapter Seven:
Other People's Margins

The Funniest Annotation I've Ever Seen

Sometimes another reader's margin note makes you laugh out loud. Record it here.

Sketch how it looked on the page.

Seen a funny margin note? Post it → #AnnotatorsOfTikTok

If Another Reader Opened My Books, They'd Say...

Imagine someone flipping through your annotated copy. What would their reaction be?

_____

_____

_____

_____

_____

_____

_____

_____

_____

_____

_____

_____

_____

Would they call you messy, brilliant, sarcastic...?

The Best Annotation I've Ever Borrowed

Have you ever copied or been inspired by someone else's annotation style? Write or draw it here.

_____

_____

_____

_____

_____

_____

Recreate their margin style.

CHAPTER EIGHT:
BOOKS THAT BECAME
RAINBOWS

The Book I've Annotated in the Most Colours

Some books demand every shade in the highlighter pack. Which one became your rainbow?

_____

_____

_____

_____

_____

_____

Test the colours you used here.

My Favourite Page Spread From That Book

Every rainbow book has one spectacular spread.
Recreate it here.

Add the quote or page number if you like.
Show your rainbow margins → #RainbowMargins

The Rainbow Effect I'd Like to Try Next

Maybe ombré highlights, pastel shading, or colour-coding moods. Describe or sketch it.

_____

_____

_____

_____

_____

_____

Sketch or swatch it here.

CHAPTER NINE:
COLLECTOR'S PAGES

My Five Favourite Annotated Quotes of All Time

Some notes deserve a hall of fame. Copy down the ones you're proudest of here.

Quote #1

Quote #2

Quote #3

Quote #4

Quote #5

A Dream Margin Design I Want to Try ☾✦

Maybe a vine of flowers, a galaxy border, or layered highlights. Sketch or describe it here.

_____

_____

_____

_____

_____

_____

Your Hall of Fame annotation → #MarginaliaMania

My Margin Signature

Every annotator has a telltale style. What makes your margins "yours"?

_____

_____

_____

_____

_____

_____

Recreate your signature style here.

CHAPTER TEN:
LEGACY IN THE MARGINS

What Future Readers Will Learn About Me

If someone picked up my annotated book years from now, what would they discover?

_____

_____

_____

_____

_____

_____

_____

_____

_____

_____

_____

_____

_____

Your notes are part of the story.

Why I Annotate

Some do it to study, some to argue, some to love a book more deeply. Why do you do it?

_____

_____

_____

_____

_____

_____

Sketch an image or symbol that represents your why.

A Message to Future Annotators

Imagine leaving advice or encouragement to the next reader who dares to write in the margins.

Dear future reader, _____

_____

_____

_____

_____

_____

_____

_____

_____

_____

_____

_____

Sign it if you want!

Pass it on: advice to future annotators → #MyMarginNotes

Notes Pages

"A room without books is like a body without a soul." — *Cicero*

The Fan's Pocket Journal Series:

The Marginalia Fan's Pocket Journal

The Magic Academy Fan's Pocket Journal

The #BookTalk & #BookGram Fan's Pocket Journal

The Romantasy Fan's Pocket Journal

. . . and many more!

Thanks for leaving your mark.
May your margins always tell a story.

White space is wasted space, so keep scribbling!

Every note in the margin is a conversation across time.

Your thoughts deserve to live beside the words that move you.

YOUR VOICE CREATES THE BOOKS YOU'LL READ TOMORROW

If this book brought you joy, please leave a review on Amazon, Goodreads, or your favourite online bookstore.

Reviews aren't just words, they're signals that help other readers discover these journals. Each review also directly supports the creation of more Fan's Pocket Journals, so your voice truly shapes what comes next!

For readers who crave worlds of wonder. . .

Enter a world of secrets, quests, and hidden love. Critically acclaimed The Bitterbynde Trilogy is the fantasy romance you'll never forget.

Secrets, quests, and love entwined

THE
BITTERBYNDE TRILOGY
The fantasy romance
critics acclaim

Available in all good bookstores

Readers who thrive on unforgettable stories will find The Bitterbynde Trilogy impossible to resist. Acclaimed by critics, it combines the lush worldbuilding of fantasy with the emotional depth of romance, pulling you into a landscape where secrets, quests, and hidden identities keep every page alive with discovery.

Its language is rich yet accessible, rewarding those who savor beautiful prose while still delivering a plot that drives forward.

For anyone who loves books that not only entertain but linger in the imagination, this trilogy is the kind you don't just read, you inhabit.

The Bitterbynde Trilogy
by Cecilia Dart-Thornton

Book #1 The Ill-Made Mute
Book #2 The Lady of the Sorrows
Book #3 The Battle of Evernight